Moth balls..

Sallie [from old catalog] Kemper

MOTH BALLS

A Play in One Act

By

SALLIE KEMPER

BOSTON
WALTER H. BAKER & CO.
1918

Moth Balls

CHARACTERS

(*As originally produced May 19, 1917, by The Theatre Arts Club at The Little Theatre of the Arts and Crafts, Detroit, Mich.*)

MARY CRAIG, *a successful playwright* -	*Grace L. Ainsworth*
BETTY HUGHES, *her secretary* - - - -	*Anna Jones*
GLADYS DEANE, *an actress* - - - -	*Jane E. Tower*

TIME.—Present. PLACE.—Country home in Massachusetts.

Moth Balls

SCENE.—*Sitting-room of* MARY CRAIG'S *cottage. Center back is a door leading to the entrance hall. The right wall is broken by another door through which a bedroom may be reached and opposite this is a curtained archway opening off the dining-room. Left center back is a bay window, affording a glimpse of the beach. A table with a typewriter, three or four stiff chairs and an old-fashioned sofa comprise the furnishings of the room. It is about eleven o'clock on a bright morning in June.*

(MARY CRAIG *is discovered dictating to her secretary. She is a slender woman, in her early thirties, whose natural prettiness has been obscured by a pair of huge, horn-rimmed nose-glasses. Her hair is drawn straight back from her forehead and she wears a most unbecoming costume. Her shirt-waist and skirt are at least ten years out of date and her mannish collar is decidedly wilted.* BETTY HUGHES, *the secretary, a pretty girl of twenty, is seated before the typewriter, industriously pounding the keys.*)

MARY. What chapter are we on now?

BETTY. The thirteenth.

MARY. And we started this novel on a Friday! (*Glancing over some typewritten pages.*) Your work is very neat and accurate, Betty. I have come to depend on you tremendously. You're the best secretary I've ever had.

BETTY (*demurely*). Thank you, Cousin Mary.

(*Adjusting her spectacles,* MARY *turns her attention to her note-book.*)

MARY (*briskly*). Let's get to work now. (*Clearing her throat, she begins to dictate.*) "When Cynthia opened her big, brown eyes ——"

BETTY. Beg pardon, but they were blue in the last chapter.

MARY. Were they? Well, I have noticed that some of our best authors create heroines with changeable eyes.

BETTY. Shall I ——?

MARY. I'll revise the text later. "When Cynthia opened her big, blue eyes she saw a butterfly hovering in her open window ——"

BETTY (*looking up*). But it was December!

MARY. That's so. Better make the butterfly into a little frozen sparrow. Editors are so critical nowadays. (*Suddenly she throws down her note-book and moves toward the younger woman.*) I can't keep my mind on my work this morning. I'm too upset.

BETTY. What is worrying you?

MARY (*abruptly*). Moth balls!

BETTY. Moth balls ——?

MARY. Don't be a parrot, my dear. (*She begins to walk nervously up and down.*) I had a letter from your Cousin John this morning.

BETTY (*in surprise*). John ——? Your husband ——?

MARY. Yes. And he chose to rake me over the coals simply because I failed to pack his fur coat away in moth balls. He says it's ruined.

BETTY. Too bad.

MARY (*leaning forward with a sudden air of confidence*). We have had two previous scenes on this subject. John thinks I neglect him terribly because I don't spend my life darning his socks, sewing on buttons for him and keeping the moths out of his clothes.

BETTY. If I had a husband as attractive as Cousin John those are just the things I'd enjoy doing for him.

MARY. Would you? Well, I'd rather write plays and

books. I'm tired of John's constant demands on me and I think I could do much better work if I were—were free!

(*Drawing a long breath.*)

BETTY (*in a little shocked voice*). Oh, Cousin Mary!

MARY. It's true. There is nothing as important as my career and John is hampering me.

BETTY. But if John——

MARY. I know John simply worships me,—and I don't like to hurt him. (*After a moment.*) But I've got to regain my independence. I can't be continually harassed by trivial things like——

BETTY (*softly*). Moth balls.

MARY (*passing her hand across her sleek, dark head in her characteristic gesture of impatience*). It's tragic,—and absurd. I won't stand it.

BETTY. But if Cousin John loves you so——

MARY. He has never even looked at any other woman. Perhaps he would do something desperate if I should leave him! (*With a genuine expression of distress.*)

BETTY (*leaning across the table with an abrupt change of manner*). For how many summers have you been coming to this cottage in Massachusetts, Cousin Mary?

MARY. This is my second season. Why?

BETTY (*brushing a blond curl out of her eyes*). Are you known as Mary Craig, the famous writer, or——?

MARY. Very few people here know that I am Mrs. John Waring. You see, John hates Gloucester and never comes to the place. He says there's nobody here but old maids and cranks.

BETTY (*chuckling*). I guess he's right.

MARY (*with an indignant glance*). What!

BETTY (*hastily*). I didn't mean that the way it sounded.

MARY (*gathering up her papers from the table. A little pause has ensued after* BETTY'S *blunder*). I am expecting Miss Gladys Deane, the famous actress, this morning, and I hope you will be particularly polite to her.

BETTY (*surprised*). Gladys Deane is coming *here?*

MARY (*nodding*). She wishes to talk over some points in my play which she is to produce next fall. I consider her the most charming actress on our stage to-day. They say that—— (*She is interrupted by the sound of the door-bell.*) Will you please see who that is, Betty? I have sent Hannah to the post-office for our mail.

(BETTY *rises and leaves the room with her customary unhurried step. A moment later she ushers in,* C. *back,* GLADYS DEANE, *a handsome, modishly dressed woman in her late twenties, whose manner is a trifle too assured.*)

MISS DEANE (*giving* MARY *a limp hand*). So glad to see you again, Miss Craig.

MARY. You haven't changed a particle! May I present my cousin, Betty Hughes? Betty—Miss Deane.

MISS DEANE (*extending the tips of her fingers to* BETTY). How do you do? (*To* MARY.) Sorry if I'm late, but it's quite a walk from my hotel here and the sun is hot.

MARY (*bringing forward a chair*). Won't you have a glass of water—or iced tea?

MISS DEANE (*sinking into the chair and fanning herself languidly*). No, thank you. I'm just a little out of breath.

MARY (*forcibly struck by the actress' languid beauty and the perfection of her attire*). You are the most ornamental woman I ever saw, Miss Deane. To look at you no one would ever suspect the prodigious amount of work of which you are capable.

MISS DEANE (*smiling*). I've been on the stage ever since I can remember and it's been nothing but hard work all the time. I'm thinking of retiring.

MARY (*taking a step backward in her amazement*). You're thinking of leaving the stage! Oh, you can't mean that.

MISS DEANE. But I do! I want to rest and enjoy life like other people.

BETTY (*demurely*). Perhaps Miss Deane expects to—to marry and settle down.

MISS DEANE (*quizzically*). Perhaps!

MARY. And what will become of my farce, "The Bandbox"?

MISS DEANE. Turn it into a musical comedy and I'll see that it's produced.

MARY. Surely you aren't thinking of leaving the stage immediately!

MISS DEANE. N-no, not immediately. (*Lowering her voice.*) I'll let you into the secret of my incipient romance. It began only last week.

BETTY. Last week!

MARY. Don't mind the little parrot, Miss Deane. You were saying——

MISS DEANE. I have at last met a man who could interest me for the rest of my life.

MARY. He must be very clever.

MISS DEANE. He is clever, handsome, amusing and—attached!

BETTY. Attached!

MARY (*frowning*). My cousin is a good example of the ancient Greek chorus.

BETTY. Pardon me. I won't interrupt again.

MISS DEANE. You mustn't think the man I refer to is in any sense a married flirt. He is too good and honest for that.

MARY. His wife——?

MISS DEANE (*a line appearing between her brows*). She forced him to indifference by her neglect. She leaves him alone for months at a time, he says, and refuses to look after his comfort in any way. I understand she made quite a scene not long ago just because he asked her to put his fur coat away in moth balls.

BETTY (*with a gasp of astonishment*). Fur coat! Moth balls! Oh, my goodness!

(*She giggles hysterically and then clapping her handkerchief over her mouth, runs hastily from the room.* MISS DEANE *turns to look after her through her pince-nez.*)

MISS DEANE. What an extraordinary young girl!

MARY (*still in the grip of her intense surprise; she has not changed her position*). Did I understand you to say this young man is deeply interested in you?

MISS DEANE. Well, not *deeply* interested. But he is lonely and susceptible. I dare say I could make him like me better—if he were free.

MARY (*a shocked note in her voice*). He is not thinking of leaving his wife——! Oh, how dreadful!

MISS DEANE. But from what John says——

MARY (*casually*). John——?

MISS DEANE. John Waring is my friend's name. He comes from a small town in Virginia. But you are entirely too famous to have ever heard of him.

(*There is a little pause.*)

MARY (*with an effort*). When did you see him last?

MISS DEANE. Yesterday. He is staying at Magnolia and we had a charming luncheon together. You can't imagine how entertaining he is.

MARY. Indeed?

MISS DEANE. Of course our attitude was entirely friendly and proper. We were chaperoned by an elderly cousin of John's. Mr. Barbour——

MARY. Did he——

MISS DEANE. The nice old dandy confided to me that John's wife is a dowdy little frump,—plain as the proverbial pipe-stem,—and is several years older than John.

MARY. That isn't so——

MISS DEANE (*astonished*). I beg your pardon!

MARY (*confused*). I said—is that so?

MISS DEANE. Well, I mustn't bore you with my personal affairs any longer.

MARY (*in a stifled voice*). You aren't—boring me.

MISS DEANE (*opening her vanity case, she begins powdering her nose*). Shall we talk about the disposal of your play?

MARY. If to-morrow would be as convenient——

MISS DEANE (*nodding*). Very well. I haven't much time to spare now as I am due in Magnolia at one for luncheon——

(*She rises, drawing on her long gloves just as the door opens and* BETTY *enters.*)

BETTY. You are wanted on the telephone, Miss Deane.

MISS DEANE (*moving toward the door with alacrity*). Thank you. You'll excuse me a moment, Miss Craig?

MARY. Certainly.

BETTY. You'll find the 'phone on the little table in the hallway. (*As the actress leaves the room,* BETTY *goes quickly to* MARY, *who has dropped her face in her hands.*) What's the matter, Cousin Mary?

MARY (*brushing the back of her hand across her eyes*). Miss Deane is b-beautiful, c-clever and c-charming—and I—I'm a fool!

BETTY (*fearing that her cousin is on the verge of hysterics*). Brace up, Cousin Mary. Don't cry. Remember you said ——

MARY (*standing up abruptly*). Never mind what I said. Where is your box that came from Altman's this morning?

BETTY. It's in my room. Why? (MARY *leaves the room* R. *precipitately without replying and a second later* MISS DEANE *returns.*) Cousin Mary wishes you to excuse her for a few minutes, Miss Deane.

(*She seats herself before her typewriter and* MISS DEANE *resumes her old place by the table. There is a little pause.*)

MISS DEANE. This seems to be the warmest day we have had.

BETTY (*absently*). Does it?

MISS DEANE. Don't you think so?

BETTY. Why, yes, I suppose ——

(MISS DEANE *yawns.*)

MISS DEANE. It will probably rain before evening.

BETTY. Probably.

(MISS DEANE *moves toward the window and stands looking out across the sand dunes.*)

MISS DEANE. What a beautiful view you have from here.

BETTY. Yes, it is nice.

(*Suddenly* MISS DEANE *approaches* BETTY *and puts a hand on her shoulder.*)

MISS DEANE. How long has your cousin been married?

BETTY (*in surprise*). *You* know that she is married?

MISS DEANE. Yes, of course.

BETTY. But as a—a friend of John's——

MISS DEANE (*smiling*). I am going to marry John Waring's *brother.*

BETTY. You are going to marry—Claud?

MISS DEANE. Yes.

BETTY (*trying to readjust herself*). And you are not—interested in John?

MISS DEANE. Only in the way that the humane society would interest itself in a stray cat. I couldn't bear to see my future brother-in-law neglected and miserable, so I thought if I came here I could *frighten* Mary out of her selfishness.

BETTY (*impulsively*). I'm glad you came,—glad you are to be a member of our family.

MISS DEANE (*kissing her*). Thank you, dear. Of course I may not have done any good to-day, but perhaps if my little bark is ever in danger of the shoals some one will help me steer clear of them. (*Picking up her parasol.*) You won't give me away to your cousin just yet, will you?

BETTY. No, indeed. But you're not going?

MISS DEANE. I've barely time to make the twelve-forty train for New York.

BETTY. John is——

MISS DEANE. With his uncle at Magnolia. Please tell "Mrs. Waring" I'm sorry I couldn't wait any longer. Perhaps I'll see you in New York this summer.

BETTY. I—I hope so.

MISS DEANE. Good-bye, then,—Betty. I may call you that?

BETTY. If you will,—Cousin Gladys. Perhaps you'll write to me? (MISS DEANE *nods and walks briskly out of the room. There is a shade of wistfulness in* BETTY'S *expression as she comes back from the entrance-hall.*

Suddenly the bedroom door opens and MARY *comes in. Her appearance is completely changed. Her hair has been fluffed out about her ears, the disfiguring spectacles are gone and her mannish costume has been replaced by a modish gown which seems to typify the essence of femininity. She wears a smart hat and carries a pink parasol.* BETTY *stares at her in amazement.*) This can't be you ——?

MARY (*breathlessly*). What's the matter with me?

BETTY. You look so different,—so pretty!

MARY. I borrowed some of your clothes. Hope you don't mind.

BETTY (*drawing a long breath*). Of course not! You look like a débutante!

MARY (*tersely*). Thanks.

BETTY. You seem entirely too young to be the well-known woman writer whose distinguished career ——

MARY (*interrupting vehemently*). Damn my career!

(*She moves quickly toward the door at back.*)

BETTY. Where are you going?

MARY. I'll take a short cut to Magnolia so as to meet my husband before that—that vampire gets to him.

BETTY. And then ——?

MARY. I'll let John see what a " dowdy old frump " he married. If he decides to give me another chance I'll show him how well I can look after his comfort.

BETTY. Aren't you going to write any more?

MARY. Yes,—but John comes first from now on. Oh, Betty, I can make him happy,—if he'll let me. He shall see me just reveling in an atmosphere of darning cotton, home-made preserves and—and moth balls!

(*She goes out quickly and* BETTY *is laughing softly to herself as she closes the door.*)

CURTAIN

STEP LIVELY

A Comedy in Two Acts

By Gladys Ruth Bridgham

Four males, ten females. Scenery, one interior; costumes, modern. Plays two hours. Billings, banker and mill owner, ruined by the war, feigns illness and keeps to his room to avoid explanations. His sister turns up with three daughters, all bringing new complications, and things come pretty swift for Billings and his son Joe. His niece, Jerusha, a born detective, opportunely turns up, however, and does some Sherlock Holmes work on a very interesting and complicated situation, and brings matters to a highly satisfactory conclusion. Very rapid and exciting; can be recommended.

Price, 25 cents

CHARACTERS

JOSEPH BILLINGS, *mill owner and President of Benham Trust Co.*
JOSEPH BILLINGS, JR., *his son.*
THEODORE CUNNINGHAM, *his secretary.*
HORATIUS THIMPLE.
MARY SMYTHE, *Billings' sister.*
BEVERLY SMYTHE, JULIET SMYTHE, ROSE-MARIE SMYTHE, *her daughters.*
GWENDOLYN SMITH, *her niece.*
MARTHA HOLTON, *Billings' niece.*
LUCILLE LOVELAND, *of the "Winsome Winnie Co."*
CARRY ARRY.
NORA, *the maid.*
JERUSHA BILLINGS.

JOHNNY'S NEW SUIT

A Comedy in Two Acts

By Mary G. Balch

Two males, five females. Scenery, interiors; costumes, modern. Plays fifty minutes. Mrs. Larkin tries to make Johnny a new suit to wear at the prize speaking competition, but does not get it further along than basting when the hour arrives. She takes a chance on the basting thread holding, but in the excitement of the occasion the threads break and Johnny's efforts are somewhat complicated. He wins out, however. Howlingly funny and strongly recommended.

Price, 25 cents

DINNER AT SEVEN SHARP

A Comedy in One Act

By Amabel and Tudor Jenks

Five males, three females. Scene, an interior; costumes, modern. Plays forty minutes. Beverly, a patent lawyer, custodian of certain papers important to a rival of the electric company that he represents, baffles, after an exciting experience, an emissary of his opponents, who is in his own employ disguised as an English butler. Very interesting and well recommended.

Price, 25 cents

THE DISTRICT ATTORNEY

A Comedy Drama in Three Acts

By Orrin E. Wilkins

Ten males, six females. Costumes, modern; scenery, two easy interiors. Plays a full evening. Bob Kendrick, college athlete and popular man, is in love with Dorothy Seabury, but she will not hear him until he has made a start in life. He runs for the office of District Attorney as part of a political trick of the "boss," Sullivan, but turns the trick and wins the election. His first official act is the prosecution of the Packing Company of which Dorothy's father is the head, which leads to his suicide and Dorothy's alienation. Later, when she knows that his strict pursuit of duty has not spared his own father's name, which was involved in the same scandal, she understands and forgives him. The political thread on which is strung a strong and varied story, introducing lots of comedy and a strong college flavor. Good enough for any purpose; strongly recommended.

Price, 25 cents

CHARACTERS

MR. WM. SEABURY, *Pres. of Seabury Packing Co.*
MR. HERBERT BROWNELL, *reporter of the "Tribune."*
RICHARD SEABURY, *senior at college.*
BOB KENDRICK, *a fixture at the university.*
BILLY REYNOLDS, *freshman at college.*
P. HOMER SULLIVAN, *politician.*
JOHN J. CROSBY, *district attorney, running for reëlection.*
JIMMIE, *office boy.*
HOWARD CALVERT, *Beverly's little brother.*
SAM, *Calvert's butler.*
AUNT HATTIE, *Wm. Seabury's sister.*
DOROTHY SEABURY, *Wm. Seabury's daughter.*
BEVERLY CALVERT, }
PEGGY MARSHALL, } *Dorothy's chums.*
POLLY WHITNEY, }
MARGARET, *servant.*

SYNOPSIS

ACT I. Drawing-room of the Seabury residence.
ACT II. The district attorney's office, a few months later.
ACT III. Same as Act I, one year later.

A SUFFRAGETTE TOWN MEETING

An Entertainment in One Act

By Lilian Clisby Bridgham

Twenty female characters. Costumes, modern; scenery, an ordinary room or hall—unimportant. Plays one hour. Presents a town meeting as it will be conducted by and by when the ladies have taken full charge of the public business. A shrewd and good-natured satire of present feminine peculiarities applied to this problem written for laughing purposes only. Just the thing for women's clubs.

Price, 25 cents

A FOUL TIP

A Comedy Drama in Three Acts

By Charles S. Allen

Seven males, three females. Costumes, modern; scenery, one exterior scene, not changed. Plays two hours. The safe at Irving's factory is robbed and three persons are under suspicion, which finally settles most strongly on Verne Gale, the hero, who, to protect Hal Irving, old Irving's son, whom his sister Nellie loves and whom he believes to be the real culprit, keeps his mouth shut save for protesting his own innocence. "Uncle" Tim Purdy is loyal to him and, with the aid of Pete Adams, the colored pitcher of the Westvale nine, finally discovers the real culprit. A strong play with unusual strength and variety of character and abundance of humorous lines and incidents. Very highly recommended.

Price, 25 cents

CHARACTERS

TIM PURDY, *postmaster, chief of police and storekeeper at Westvale.*
HIRAM ROWELL, *the village expressman.*
OLIVER IRVING, *manufacturer.*
HAROLD IRVING, *his son.*
VERNE GALE, *manager of the Westvale nine.*
POLLARD, *Irving's bookkeeper.*
PETE ADAMS, *colored pitcher on the Westvale nine.*
ALMIRA PURDY, *Tim's wife.*
MABEL REMINGTON, *Irving's stenographer.*
NELLIE GALE, *Verne's sister.*
Members of the ball team, villagers, etc.

DADDY

A Comedy in Three Acts

By Lilli Huger Smith

Four males, four females. Costumes, modern; two easy interiors. Plays an hour and a half. Mr. Brown exhausts all the resources of science, including smallpox and diphtheria signs, in an endeavor to keep away the admirers of his daughter whom he wishes to keep at home. He finally asks Dr. Chester, who is privately in love with her, to help him to dissuade her from becoming a trained nurse. The doctor does so by marrying her himself. Very clever and amusing; full of wit and of high tone. Strongly recommended.

Price, 25 cents

CHARACTERS

MR. WREXSON BROWN, *just like his fellow men.*
TEDDY BROWN, *his son, pursuing football at college.*
PAUL CHESTER, *a young doctor.*
THOMPSON, *the Browns' butler.*
MRS. WREXSON BROWN, *just like her fellow women.*
NELLIE BROWN, *her daughter, a débutante.*
MRS CHESTER, *Mr. Brown's sister, pursuing ill-health at home.*
JANE, *the Browns' cook.*

RED ACRE FARM

A Rural Comedy Drama in Three Acts by Gordan V. May. Seven males, five females. Costumes, modern; scenery, one interior, one exterior. Plays two hours. An easy and entertaining play with a well-balanced cast of characters. The story is strong and sympathetic and the comedy element varied and amusing. Barnaby Strutt is a great part for a good comedian; "Junior" a close second. Strongly recommended.

Price, 25 cents

THE COUNTRY MINISTER

A Comedy Drama in Five Acts by Arthur Lewis Tubbs. Eight males, five females. Costumes, modern; scenery not difficult. Plays a full evening. A very sympathetic piece, of powerful dramatic interest; strong and varied comedy relieves the serious plot. Ralph Underwood, the minister, is a great part, and Roxy a strong soubrette; all parts are good and full of opportunity. Clean, bright and strongly recommended.

Price, 25 cents

THE COLONEL'S MAID

A Comedy in Three Acts by C. Leona Dalrymple. Six males, three females. Costumes, modern; scenery, two interiors. Plays a full evening. An exceptionally bright and amusing comedy, full of action; all the parts good. Capital Chinese low comedy part; two first-class old men. This is a very exceptional piece and can be strongly recommended.

Price, 25 cents

MOSE

A Comedy in Three Acts by C. W. Miles. Eleven males, ten females. Scenery, two interiors; costumes, modern. Plays an hour and a half. A lively college farce, full of the true college spirit. Its cast is large, but many of the parts are small and incidental. Introduces a good deal of singing, which will serve to lengthen the performance. Recommended highly for co-educational colleges. *Price, 15 cents*

OUR WIVES

A Farce in Three Acts by Anthony E. Wills. Seven males, four females. Costumes, modern; scenery, two interiors. Plays two hours and a half. A bustling, up-to-date farce, full of movement and action; all the parts good and effective; easy to produce; just the thing for an experienced amateur club and hard to spoil, even in the hands of less practical players. Free for amateur performance. *Price, 25 cents*

THE SISTERHOOD OF BRIDGET

A Farce in Three Acts by Robert Elwin Ford. Seven males, six females. Costumes, modern; scenery, easy interiors. Plays two hours. An easy, effective and very humorous piece turning upon the always interesting servant girl question. A very unusual number of comedy parts; all the parts good. Easy to get up and well recommended. *Price, 25 cents*

S. J. PARKHILL & CO., PRINTERS, BOSTON, U.S.A.